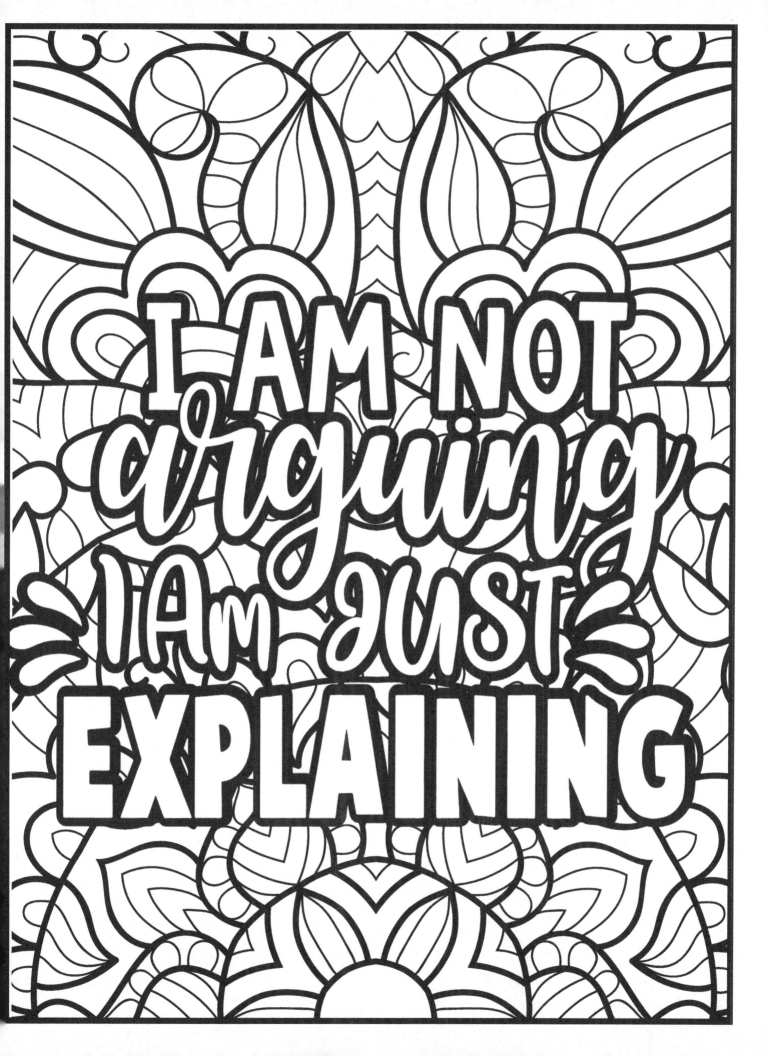

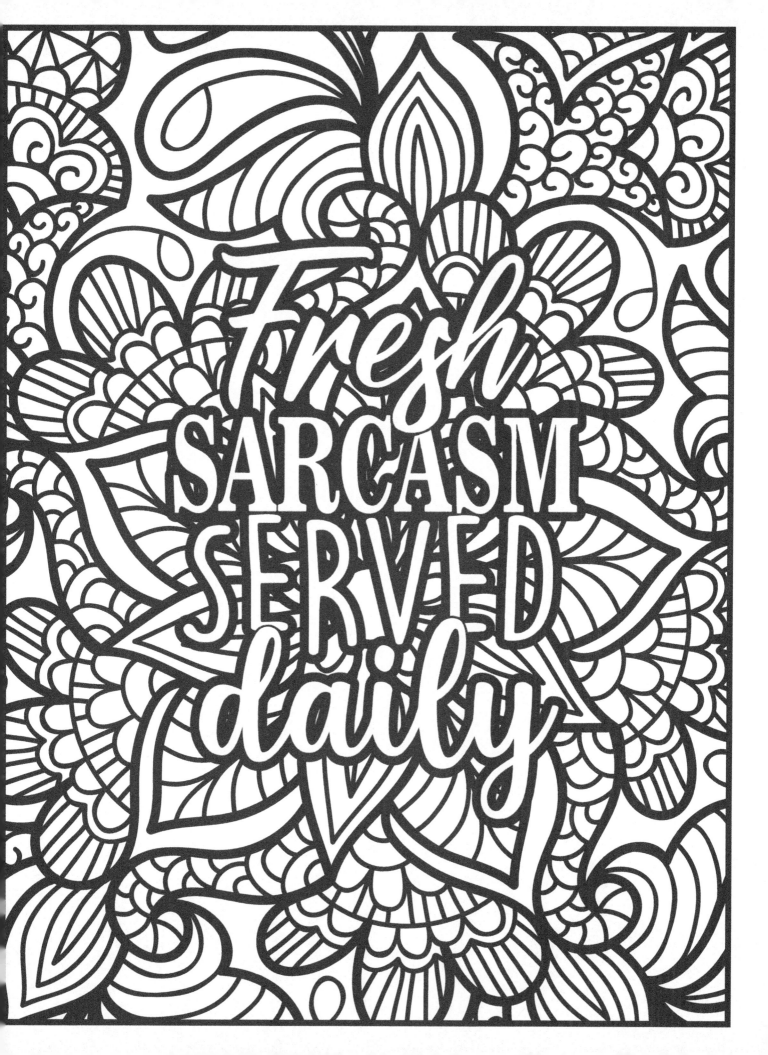

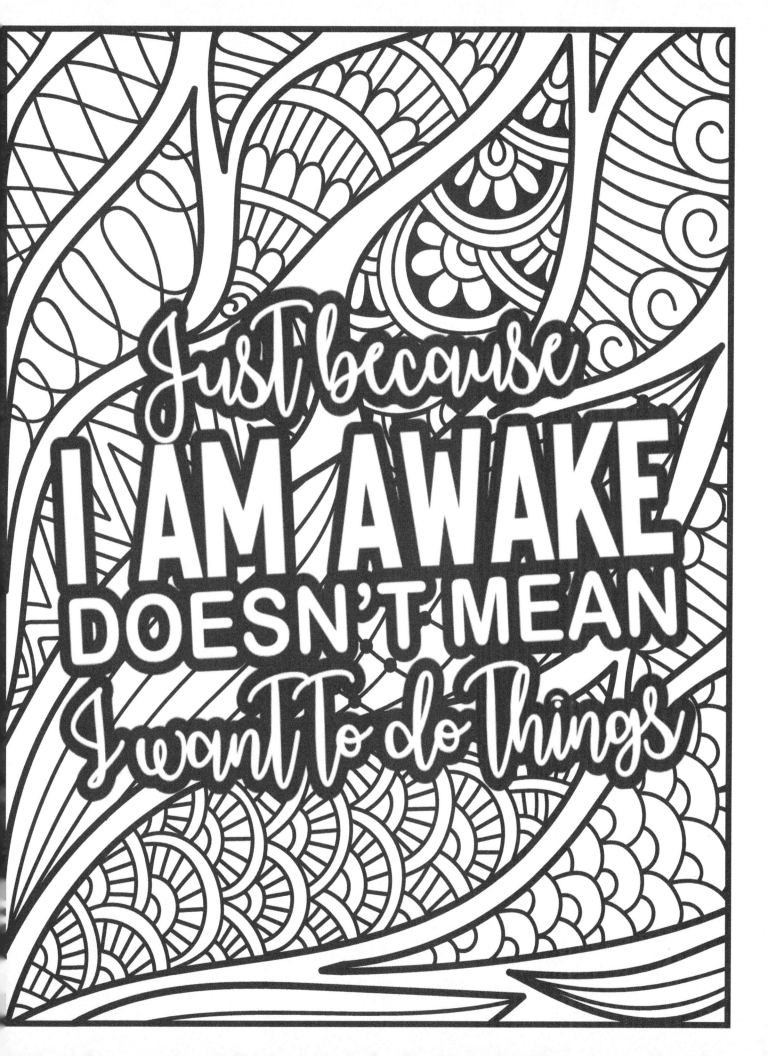

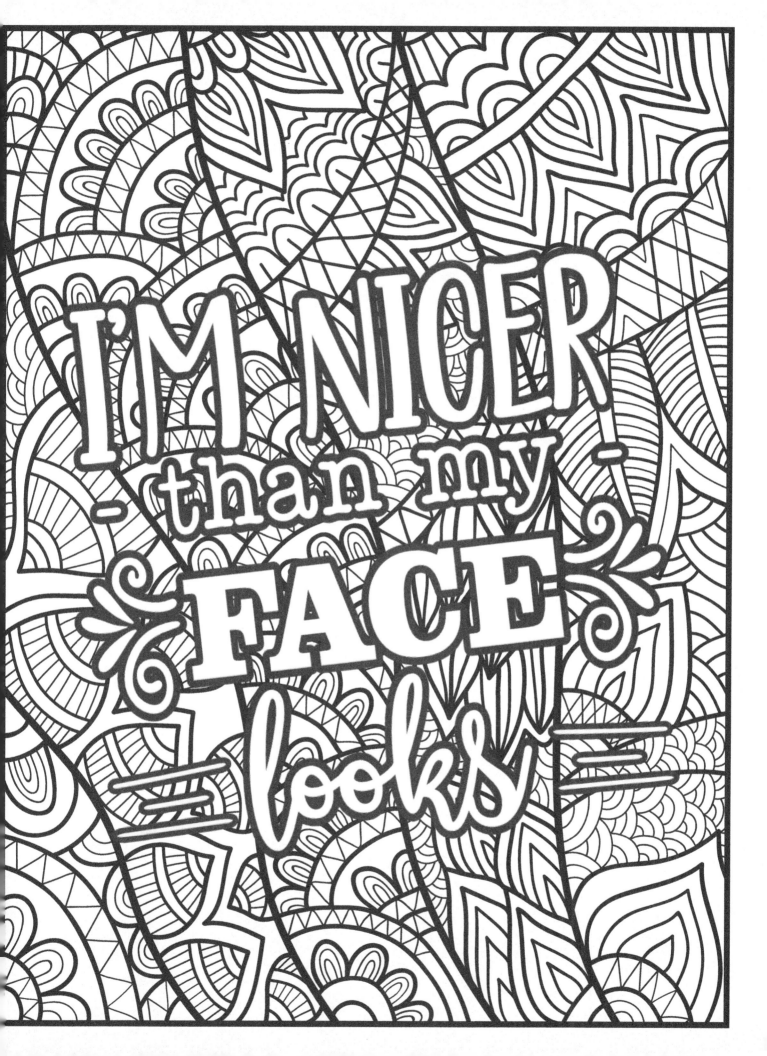

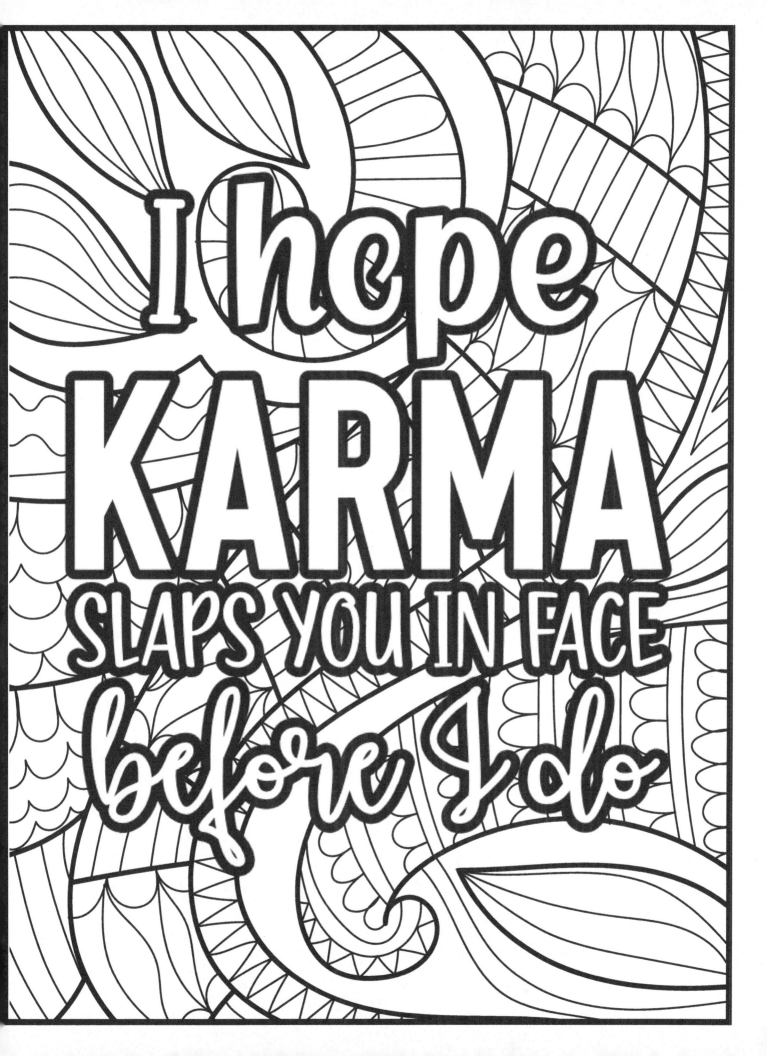

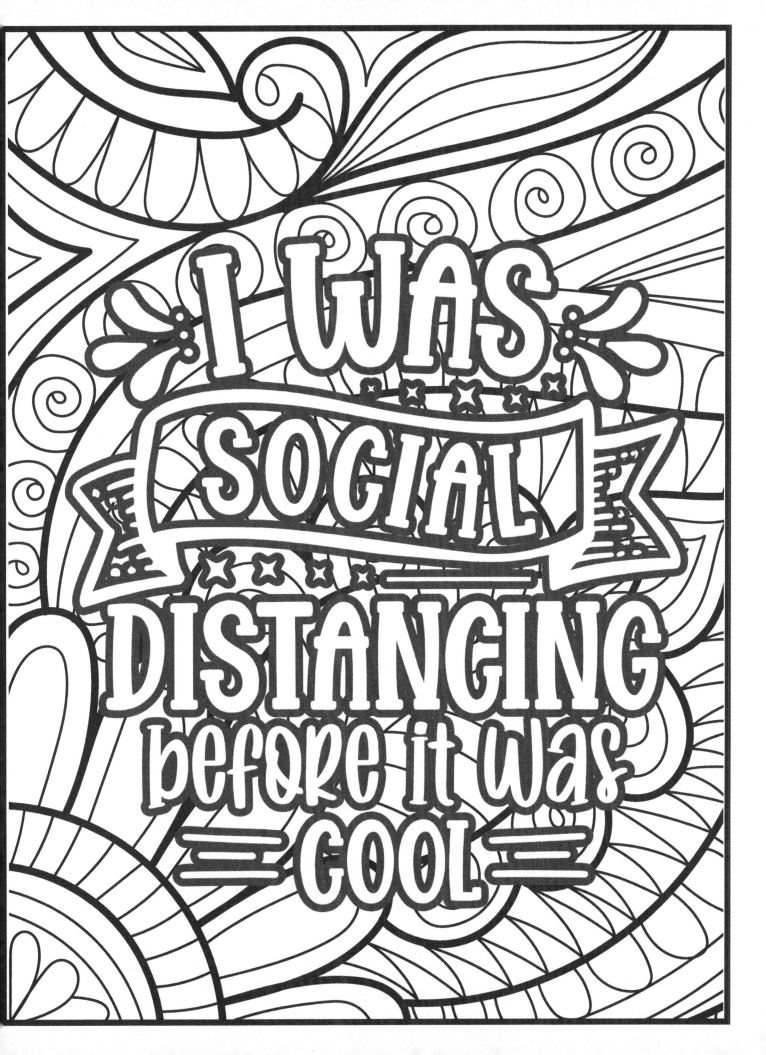

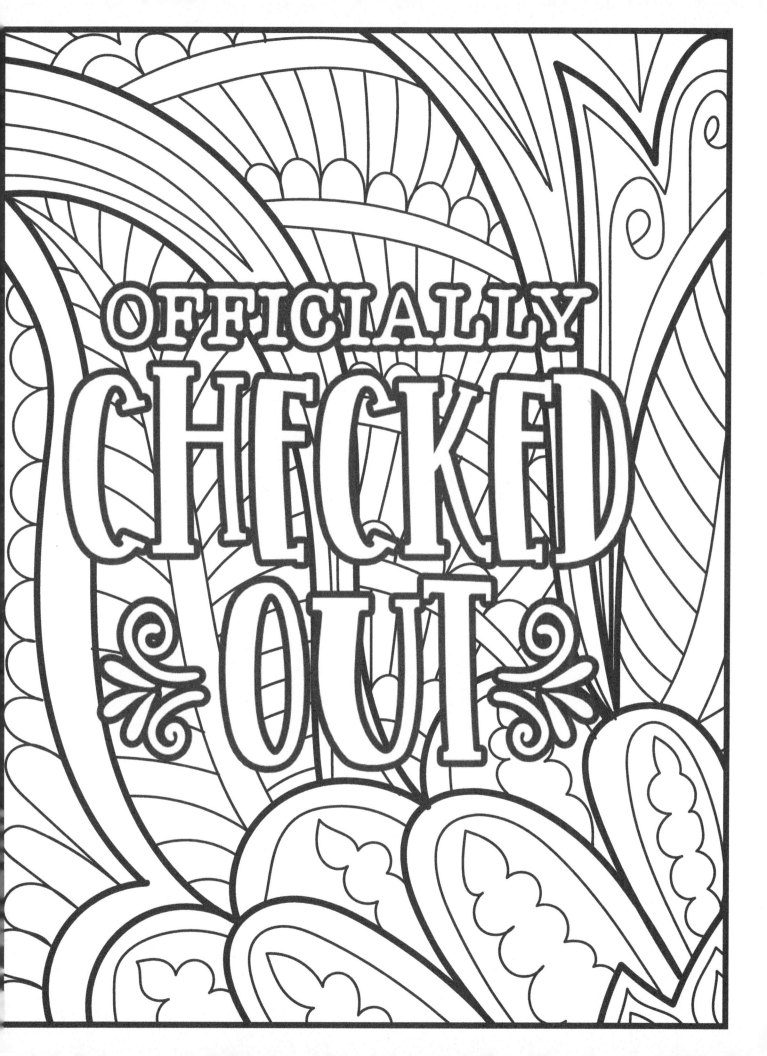

Just One More Thing!

Reviews are an important part of any book's success. It would mean a lot to me if you would take a moment to leave an honest rating or review of this book.

Thanks so much!

PS May I suggest putting a piece of paper underneath the page you're coloring to prevent bleed through? There's a couple of blank pages at the back of this book, just in case you need them.

Or, why not use them to doodle a few sarcastic thoughts of your own?

COLOR TESTER

Use the squares below to test your shading and colors.

COLOR TESTER

Use the squares below to test your shading and colors.

Made in the USA
Coppell, TX
12 November 2024

40090438R00044